Amazon FBA Sales Boost

33 Little Tricks to Increase Your Amazon Private Label Sales, Get Organic Free Traffic, and Create a More Profitable FBA Ecommerce Business

[Amazon FBA Business Series – Part 5]

Red Mikhail

TABLE OF CONTENTS

Title, Keywords, Description, Features, Seller Feedback, Brand Registry, the Buy Box, Product Classification, etc.

Value Skewing, Product Inserts, Product Differentiation, Purchase Add-Ons, Variety, Product Options, etc.

Amazon PPC, Facebook Ads, Instagram Influencers, Reviewers Program, Lightning Deals, etc.

Introduction

Welcome to part 5 of the Fulfillment by Amazon business series. In this book, I am going to show you 33 different ways to boost your FBA sales. If you're not familiar with this type of business yet, then I highly recommend that you read at least part 1 and part 2 of the series' first. Those 2 books (Amazon FBA step by step and FBA Product Research 101) will give you a great foundation on how you can get started with Amazon FBA.

Just like my other books, you should expect a straight to the point, no B.S. kind of guide. I won't bore you with useless details and I definitely don't need to tell you my life story. If you've been reading my books for a while now, then you already know that I go straight to the actionable and important stuff.

If you're the type of person who hates fluff, then this book is for you.

Overview

When most people think about AMAZON SALES, they only think about the marketing part. They think about product promotions and advertising. The truth is, marketing is only a third of the process. When it comes to Amazon ecommerce sales, you have to think about the following:

Optimization, Product, and Marketing.

Optimization is about maximizing the tools that you have at your disposal. These are things like product titles, keyword research, pricing, product category, etc.

Think of optimization as your most low effort foundational work that will have a surprisingly big impact on your sales. If you don't believe what I'm saying then try it out for yourself. Create 2 similar listings: One applying the lessons from this book and the other ignoring the strategies that I will show you. I guarantee you that the first listing will do at least 2x better when it comes to sales.

Product is about making sure that your customers have options so they can have the best buying experience. This is all about giving them various choices like colors, sizes, quality of materials, etc. This part discusses the concept of "value skewing" and how it can help you dominate your market by having a superior product.

Marketing is about using the right medium to promote your products. Mediums like Amazon PPC, Facebook Ads, Instagram Marketing, Lightning Deals, Amazon's Reviewer Program, etc. This is what people usually think about when it comes to increasing sales. But as you already know, this is only 1/3 of the whole pie. I bet that you'll easily increase your sales by at least 50% even if you only applied part 1 and part 2 of this training. In part 3, I'll show you the best practices to follow so you can maximize these promotion platforms and increase your sales even more.

Some of the ideas are easy to implement and then there are some that will take more time and effort to do. One idea may not get you the amount of sales you are aiming for, but when combined, can boost your sales up to more than 100% of what you currently have right now.

I don't necessarily think that you have to apply each and every one of the ideas. However, I do hope that you'll implement at least 20% of what you'll read. I promise you, doing that alone will do wonders to your FBA business.

Here's my best recommendation for you. Suspend your disbelief for a moment, read every single page of this book, and then choose something that resonates with you.

I'm super excited that you're here, let's get started, shall we?

Part 1

Optimization Ideas

Sales Boost Idea #1 - Optimize Your Title

I will tell you straight up that your title is the most important text in your listing. It could literally be the difference between $100 months and $1,000 months. Why? Because your title tells Amazon and the customers what your product is. Remember, since Amazon is a search engine for products, the customers are looking for the exact product that will either:

A – Solve their problem

B – Fulfill their needs or wants

If your title doesn't fully indicate that it is the product that the customers need, then there's no way they would even click at your listing.

Another important thing to remember about title is that it is heavily weighted for keyword rankings. I have no idea what the exact percentage is (only Amazon knows that). But I do know that your title plays a major role when it comes to Amazon SEO and keyword rankings.

Here are some guidelines to take note of when it comes to product titles:

1 – It must not exceed 200 characters including spaces. Treat these 200 characters as if they are prime real estate and maximize their use.

2 – Do not use any promotional text like: free, sale, discounted, buy now, etc.

3 – Do not use any subjective terms like: best, fastest, most affordable, cheapest, etc. These are words that are harder to define and Amazon does frown upon sellers who uses subjective terms.

4 – Do state the quantity of the product. For example: 1 gallon, 1 liter, 5 pieces, 2 packs, etc.

5 – Do not use any special characters like: "" or *.

6 – Most importantly, do not stuff them with unrelated keywords. If your product is a guitar cord, then do not put any keyword that is unrelated to a guitar cord. I shouldn't have to say this but I see beginner sellers do this just for the sake of adding keywords. Amazon hates it when you do this. It messes up their algorithm and it gives the customers a terrible buying experience. Imagine looking for a bread maker and seeing lots of random "dog breeding" books instead. Yikes!

Here's the title formula that I recommend you follow:

Title formula: Brand Name + Primary Keyword/Product Name + Main Features (Quantity, Benefits, Uses)

Examples:

Bambino *Bamboo Toothbrush, BPA Free Soft Bristles, Eco Friendly, Compostable Toothbrushes, 10 Pieces.*

__Greener Chef__ Extra Large Bamboo Cutting Board for Kitchen, Organic Wood Butcher Block – Wooden Carving Board for Meat and Vegetables - 18 x 12.5

Make sure that you put your most important keywords in your title. These should be keywords that are getting the majority of searches according to your research.

Sales Boost Idea #2 - Target the Right Keywords for Amazon SEO

The keywords that you will use will pretty much determine whether you'll make money on Amazon or not. Why? Because Amazon is a search engine. People are looking for products directly instead of trying to find more information about something (books are the exception).

You will use these keywords for your title, description, features, Amazon keyword optimization (when you create your listing), etc.

Here's how you create a keyword list:

Step 1 - Create Master Spreadsheet. Use this file as the storage for all your keywords.

Step 2 - Use Amazon.com to search for competitors. Search for your product on Amazon and look at the top 10 results. Copy and paste the relevant keywords that you'll find.

Example:

[Image 1.1]

In this example [refer to image 1.1], the keywords that I found are:

Organic Bamboo Cutting Board
Cutting Boards
Carving Board
Chopping Board for Meat and Vegetable

Continue adding keywords to your spreadsheet until you have at least 100. Most of the time, you will find terms that'll appear over and over again. That's where we utilize a tool called Helium10.

Step 3 - Use Helium10 to rearrange keywords. Helium10 is a free tool that you can use to rearrange your keywords. You can use this to cut the fat and remove the keywords that appears over and over again. Remember, if you have keywords like: "Bamboo toothbrush" and "Bamboo toothbrushes", Amazon will automatically count the word "bamboo" as only one keyword so there's no need to repeat mentioning that keyword again and again.

Original keywords

Total characters: 11827 Total words: 1645

bamboo toothbrush
toothbrush
best toothbrush
charcoal toothbrush
kids electric toothbrush
baby toothbrush
biodegradable toothbrush
wooden toothbrush
eco toothbrush
eco friendly toothbrush
gum toothbrush

Output settings

Add only spaces   Remove duplicates
One word/phrase per line   Maintain phrases
Add commas no space   Protect numbers
Add commas with space   Convert to lowercase
Include word frequency count   Remove common words
                                   Remove single words
                                   Remove single letters

[Image 1.2]

Use the following output setting:

1 – One word/phrase per line
2 – Remove duplicates
3 – Convert to lower case

Then on the right side of the original keyword section, click on **frequency**.

When you look at your keywords, you will see the most frequent keywords that are searched over and over again.

Most likely, the first 5-10 results are your main keywords. They are the keywords where more than 40% of your traffic will come from if you're on the first page of Amazon for those keywords.

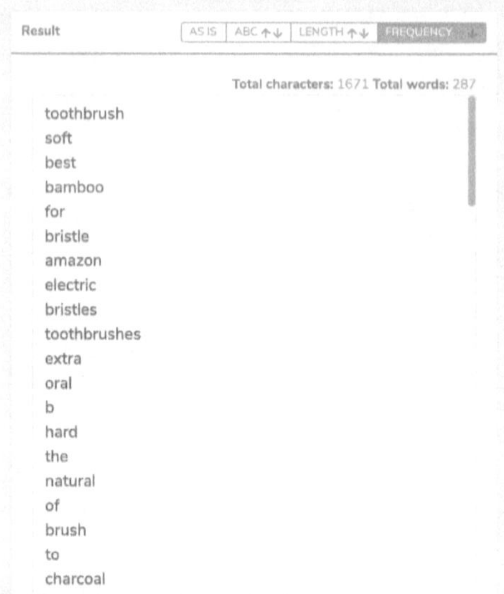

[Image 1.3]

The next step is to browse your list and look for non-relevant keywords that you can remove.

Remove the keywords that has nothing to do with your product.

Once you're done with that step, just click the "Add Only Spaces" in the output settings to re-arrange your keywords.

The results are your main keywords that you can use for your titles, description, features, etc.

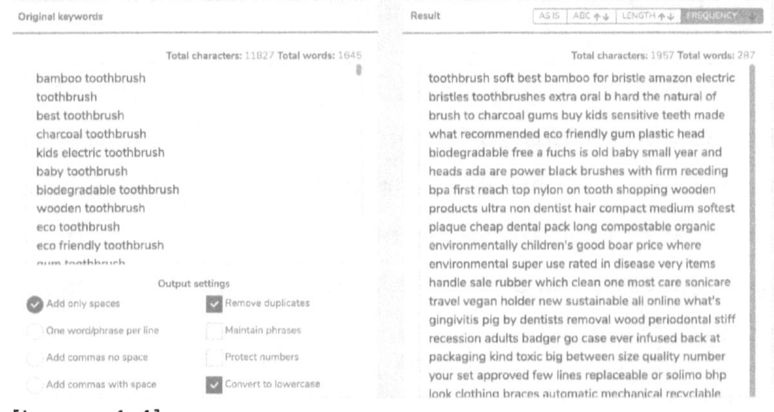

[Image 1.4]

The final step is to click save which lets you download the list as a text file.

If you want to find out more and go in depth on keyword research (without spending any money on tools), I recommend that you check out my book Amazon Keyword Research.

https://www.amazon.com/gp/product/B08JHGWPVF

Sales Boost Idea #3 – Optimize Your Product Images

You already know how important a product image is. You probably won't buy something that looks like the photos were taken from the 50s. Instead of blabbing on how you should get professional photos (which you should be doing), let me talk about the technical aspect of Amazon product images instead.

1 – Image Priority

As of the writing of this book, Amazon allows up to 9 images for your product. Make sure that you maximize the number of allowed photos you can upload on your listing. Try different angles so the customers can look at your product with different point of views, literally speaking.

Also, assign priority to each image – that means that first 3 images that they should see are the best ones. For example, if you are selling a lawn mower – then they should see the product as a whole for the first 3 photos. Next, you can add pictures while the product is in action. See image 1.5, 1.6 and 1.7 for examples.

[Image 1.5]

[Image 1.6]

2 – Technical Image Requirements

A – Image Size: It should be at least 1,000 pixels in width or height.

B – Background Color: Only use white background when you're featuring a product.

C – File Format: Upload using JPEG, PNG, GIF or TIFF.

D – Color Mode: sRGB and CMYK are acceptable.

E – Image Frame: Your product should fill 80%-85% of the frame.

3 – Amazon-Based Standard

Only use actual photos of the product. Vectors, illustrations, drawing, graphics, and text overlays will make your listing look unprofessional.

4 – Use Variety

Try to be creative when it comes to your product images. Use different angles, show the product in action, show the packaging, add key information, and make your product as exciting as possible.

This is where a professional product photographer can help you big-time! Check out their past works before you hire somebody and make sure that they are taking professional, clean, and high-quality images.

5 – Add Key Information

For most products, you can feature some kind of key information that will make your product standout. It can be a material that you use or a key feature that makes your product one of a kind.

For example, if your bamboo toothbrush has BPA free nylon bristles and biodegradable handle, then you can also feature that on your product photos. This gives your customers more information about the item and it highlights what is so special about your product.

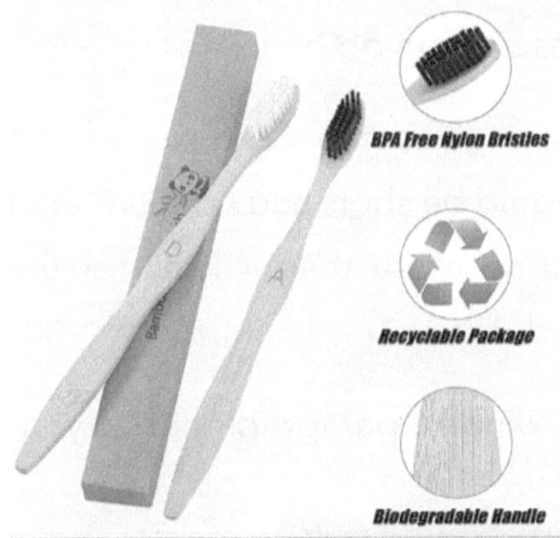

[Image 1.7]

Sales Boost Idea #4 - Improve Your Product Description

First of all, let me define what the product description IS NOT.

Product description is not the text that you see beside the product images. Those are bullet points. Product descriptions are also not the place where you duplicate and copy what you already said in the bullet points.

So, what does a product description do?

A good product description gives the **features** of the product. In my opinion, it should be short and no more than 7 lines for the features and no more than 4 lines for the technical aspects of the product.

So instead of doing a long-winded paragraph about your product:

These durable and biodegradable toothbrushes have ergonomically designed handles made from Moso bamboo and powered by medium and BPA Free Nylon bristles. So, our toothbrushes are perfect for those who care about the environment and pursue a zero waste lifestyle.

We are closer to our goal of making the Earth an eco-friendly and cruelty-free place. Moso Bamboo is one of the most sustainable resources on Earth and native to China and Taiwan. It can grow in damaged and nutrients depleted soil and due to its rapid regrowth cycle it can be harvested with virtually no environmental impact. Moso Bamboo is not eaten by Giant Pandas, which is also a good news for all panda lovers.

[Image 1.8]

You should instead do something like this: [refer to image 1.9]

☑ Has medium nylon bristles. Strong enough to offer plenty of polishing power, but gentle enough to not to cause enamel damage.

☑ Dries fast and does not absorb water. Last long as plastic toothbrushes.

☑ Comes in a recyclable box. A perfect gift for a housewarming or any eco-minded friend.

☑ Pack of 4 toothbrushes. Great for a small to medium sized family.

☑ Non-Charcoal Toothbrush

[Image 1.9]

It should be in bullet form. It should be easy & fast to read, and it should give them additional reasons to choose your product over the competition.

You can also add dimension and specs, key information they need to know, plus any warranty or guarantee that your company provides (if there's any).

Check out this example below: [refer to image 1.9]

Product description

Color: Black

This 1500W Mini Ceramic Heater from Joy Pebble utilizes industry leading ceramic heating discs for ultra-warm heat transfer in small spaces. Ceramic heating is the latest technology in mini space heaters and provides a faster, safer and more energy efficient method of heating than traditional space heaters. At the flick of switch, the ceramic fan heater will produce a stream of warm air to quickly and effectively heat the area in front of the heater.

Product description:
Product weight: 3.6 lbs
Noise: 30-40db
Color: black and white
Material: ABS plastic
Power unit: AC power supply
Volt: 110v
Watts: 750 / 1500W
Special properties: dump power off, overheat protection, adjustable power
Included: hot air blower space heater, instruction manuel
Product Dimensions: W8.9"*D6.1"*H9.4"

[Image 1.9]

For the main description, I would actually change that to a bullet point style instead of having 4-5 sentences in one paragraph. Also, take note of the "special properties or special instructions" part as you may need to let your customers know about that as well depending on the type of product that you have.

Sales Boost Idea #5 - Use Punchy Features & Bullet Points

After your title, your bullet points are the most important part of your listing. Those bullet points should be short and punchy. Meaning: They have to show the advantages of choosing your product over the other products on Amazon. In addition, they must not be bored with technical details that doesn't relate to what they really want or need. For example, if you're selling a bamboo toothbrush, then you're most likely dealing with a customer who wants to protect the earth in her own little way. In this case, you have to show her the features that actually matches her goals. You can mention that your product is BPA FREE, biodegradable, and eco-friendly.

Here's the formula that I follow when it comes to product features:

Line #1 - Feature + Benefits

The first line should give them the #1 most important benefit of the product.

Line #2 - Feature + Benefits

The 2nd line shows them the 2nd biggest benefit and feature of the product.

Line #3 – Differentiate

The next line should give them some kind of reason why your product is different from the others. This usually comes from having a product that is actually better than your competitors (I know, new concept right? Lol). You cannot fake this one, so make sure that you have a good product.

Line #4 - Twist the Knife + Solve the Problem

In the 4th line, I explain to them what problem this product solves and then I give them the solution for it.

For example, you can say that your product is 100% biodegradable which helps the earth so they don't have to worry about polluting the environment anymore.

Line #5 - Guarantees

I give them a guarantee that the product works or else they can send it back to me and get a 100% refund (mention this if you do offer some).

***

In order to follow this formula, you have to know who your customer is. You have to know their main motivation for buying a product like yours. You can usually do this research by reading the positive and negative reviews of your competitors.

If you want a shortcut on writing your bullet points, you can just read the bullet points of your most reviewed competitors and just rephrase their bullets. Look at the main points they are targeting and use them for your bullets as well.

Sales Boost Idea #6 - Add a Video to Your Amazon Listing

A note before we start. This idea is only open for owners who are already approved for the Amazon Brand Registry Program which we will discuss later.

A lot of sellers won't bother doing a video for their product because it does take some additional work on their part. Now, you don't have to do this when you launch your product but it does help in converting more customers. I recommend that you launch without it but then immediately work your butt off so you can add it on your listing as soon as possible.

Videos are great because they can show the product in flesh. You can show that a real human being is actually using the product. They also have higher retention rates and customers are more likely to buy if they are engaged through your video. Another benefit of videos is they are great for SEO. They can add a lot of traffic to your listing and you don't even have to pay for it.

Here's a few things to remember when you're doing a video for your product listing:

A – The video should show the product's features and benefits. Think of it as the video version of your bullet points.

B – When it comes to video, lighting and audio is key. Make sure that you hire a professional to shoot the video for you. You don't have to spend thousands of dollars to do this. A simple 30-second video of your product + text overlay (which mentions the features) will do.

Here's an example that you can copy:

https://www.youtube.com/watch?v=BMKjRC9r2zk&
C – Adding customer video reviews can also be a substitute.

D – You can upload your video through Amazon's Enhance Brand Content feature.

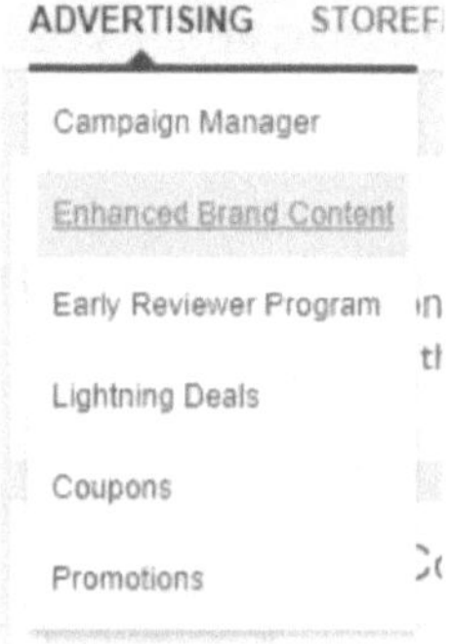

[Image 1.10]

Just follow these steps:

1 – Enter the SKU representing the ASIN of the product you want to use for EBC.

2 – Select your preferred template and fill the text and image slots.

3 – Follow the onscreen prompts and upload the following:

Video file, Image thumbnail, video title, and video description.

4 – Save the changes and submit the content for validation and approval.

Source of instruction:
https://www.sellerapp.com/help/article/add-video-amazon-listing/

Sales Boost Idea #7 - Remove Negative Seller Feedback (Review Section and Feedback Profile)

Negative feedback sucks.

It can affect your sales and how potential customers perceived your product's value. Not every negative feedback can be removed but we must try to erase them whenever possible.

So when can we request for Amazon to remove a negative feedback?

Case #1 – When customers used "obscene language" and "personally identifiable information".

You can request for that feedback to be removed if it contains R-rated language like in a movie. Would you want your kid to read this review? Would it be perfectly okay for them to see the language that was used? If not, then you can contest that feedback. In addition, you can also request to remove a review if there are some personal details that may affect you or the customer.

Case #2 – If the review has nothing to do with the product itself.

If the reviews on the product page and/or your seller profile has nothing to do with the product itself, then you can also request for it to be removed. For example, if an order is late or there has been some issues with fulfillment, then Amazon will take responsibility for that issue and will include a comment that says something like this:

"This item was fulfilled by Amazon, and we take responsibility for this fulfilment experience."

Here's how to remove negative feedback:

Option 1 – Contact Amazon

Open your seller central account and go to

Select Account Settings > Orders > Customer feedback problems.

Send a short message explaining why you think the feedback should be removed in the first place.

Here's an example message:

Hi, I've received a feedback from Alex K. on [order number] and it looks like the comment was based on unsatisfactory customer experience. Is there any way we can remove this feedback on my profile?

Here is the comment:

[Insert feedback here]

Thank you,

Red

You will receive a message that looks like this if you're successful in removing that feedback. [Refer to Image 1.11]

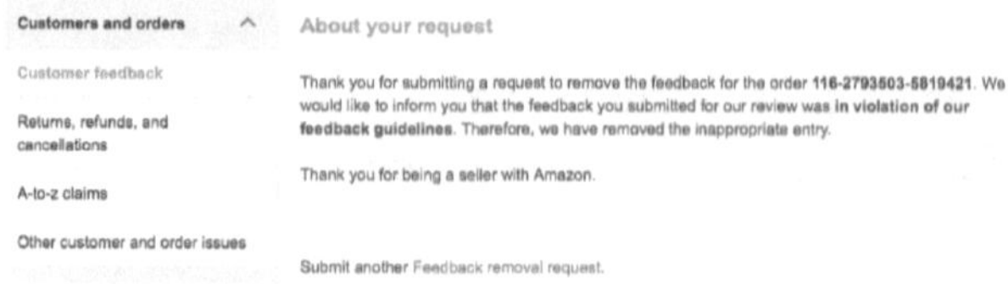

[Image 1.11]

Option 2 – Contact the Customer

Another thing that you can do is to contact the customer and ask them to remove the negative feedback.

Now, be careful because you cannot offer anything in return. It is against Amazon's terms to give a full refund or give anything in exchange for deleting the feedback.

You cannot connect the act of removing the feedback to getting a full refund.

All you can do is apologize for the unsatisfactory service/product and explain what you're doing for it to never happen again. And then humbly ask for them to remove the negative feedback.

Note: The feedback must be removed 60 days from the time they posted it or the feedback won't be eligible for removal after this timeframe.

Sales Boost Idea #8 - Optimal Pricing

It can be difficult to come up with the right price for your product. On one hand, you want to make as much profit as possible. On the other hand, you also don't want it to be super expensive that no one will buy it anymore. So finding the right price for your product may took some trial and error.

I recommend that you follow these steps when optimizing the price of your product:

Step 1 – Get a feel of the market.

The first step is to go to Amazon and just look at your competitors. How much are they selling their product? Is their product offer similar to yours or are they adding something that other seller don't have?

If everyone is selling for $12.99, then you might want to offer yours for $12.49 as a start.

Step 2 – Take note of the 5x rule.

As a general rule, I make sure that I can sell the product for at least 5x the production cost. If it cost me $2 to produce a product per piece, then I must be able to sell it on Amazon for $10. By following the 5x rule, I am giving myself some safety net to still make a decent (20-30%) net profit after all the expenses and FBA fees.

Step 3 – Don't get greedy.

You have to think long-term. Just because you can make an extra $500 per month by increasing your price by $1 doesn't mean you should do it. If you're just starting out and you don't have a lot of reviews yet, I highly recommend that you price your product for as low as possible. You should still be able to make a profit mind you, but in the beginning, the focus should be in getting reviews and building a good reputation for your brand.

Step 4 – Do 14 to 30-day tests.

When you're doing price tests, make sure that you do it in 14 to 30-day timeframes. You cannot possibly get an accurate sales data if you're changing the price every 3 days. Do these tests for 6 months and then look at the data for which price gets the most sales. (Preferably not in December since your data may get skewed by Holiday sales).

Sales Boost Idea #9 - Let Your Customers Ask Questions

Answering customers' questions is a great way to connect with them and it also allows you to remove their doubts before buying your product.

Message some of your customers and let them ask questions about your product. You can also ask a friend of yours to do this and you can show him the most important ones to ask.

Questions should be specific to the product and questions should be about capturing the experience of using the product.

For example:

- How long does this toothbrush last?
- Should I dispose it after 3 months?
- Can I connect an external mic on this camera?
- How long do I need to charge the battery?

Here are some topics that you shouldn't answer:

- Shipping or delivery
- Product availability
- Order specific information
- Customer service

Here are the instructions on asking and answering questions according to Amazon.

How do I ask a question?

On a product page, scroll to the "Customer Questions & Answers" feature. Enter your question in the text box and click "Ask".

How do I answer a question?

To answer questions, click "See all questions & answers" and choose questions you can answer from the "Unanswered questions" feature in the right column.

Have a question?

Find answers in product info, Q&As, reviews

🔍 Type your question or keyword

Customer questions & answers

🔍 Have a question? Search for answers

Question: are the bristles also biodegradable?

18 votes
Answer: So far we don't have a material which is 100% biodegradable to replace nylon. We are doing our best to make it come true. But the handle part is made of natural bamboo, it occupied more than 95% of toothbrush.
By Isshah SELLER on July 3, 2018

Question: is it BPA free?

5 votes
Answer: Yes,They are all BPA free and made from nature bamboo
By Isshah SELLER on January 7, 2019

Question: Where are these made? I don't want to buy them if they're made in a sweatshop.

5 votes
Answer: The problem is that if we do not buy because they come from a sweatshop, poor people who work at the sweatshop will run out of work. This is an issue that has to be addressed on a different way other than boycotting.
By Cavolino on April 5, 2020
▾ See more answers (1)

Question: Do the bristles fall out? I bought another brand of bamboo toothbrushes and the bristles fall out.

1 vote
Answer: I had to say this, because I like these brushes. But my bristles fell out of 2 brushes. The first one was after about a month. I felt something like a hair as I was brushing. Disgusting! But I saw it was black, and it was like a "V". So I continued brushing, then another "V", and another. They were all falling out. So ... see more
By Grandpa Chuckle on December 9, 2020
▾ See more answers (6)

[Image 1.12]

Additional Notes:

A – I highly recommend that you answer as many questions as you can.

B – Go research questions by spying on your competitors. Read their listing, their reviews, and their own Q & A section.

Sales Boost Idea #10 - Apply for Brand Registry

If you want to gain complete control over your Amazon listings, then you have to apply for Brand Registry.

Brand Registry allows you access to enhanced marketing features that Amazon provides. It helps protect a registered trademark and it helps you in having complete control over your brand's image. With Brand Registry, you can add branded products, manage them properly, and eliminate imitation which ensures that your customers are buying legit versions of that product.

Do you remember those super cool and professional product descriptions with text and images? [refer to image 1.13 for an example]. Well those are made via Enhance Brand Content which you can only access if you have Brand Registry.

[Image 1.13]

Brand Registry also allows you to win the Buy Box which we will discuss later. There's obviously a ton more benefits but I'm not going to discuss all of those here.

Just know that having **Brand Registry is a MUST.**

Here's how you apply for one:

Step 1 – Check Eligibility Requirements

This will differ from country to country, but the most basic requirements are: A Trademark, a Text-Based Trademark, and an Image-Based Trademark.

Check your requirements here:

https://brandservices.amazon.com/eligibility

Step 2 – Sign Up for Brand Registry

https://brandservices.amazon.com/eligibility

You need to input the following information:

- Give your businesses' information
- Validate your identity via SMS
- Read and accept its policies

Step 3 – Enroll Your Brand/s

Here are the 4 aspects of enrolling a brand:

1 – Brand Eligibility

This consists of your brand name, a few information about your brand, and the number of brand names you want to enroll to Enhance Brand Content (EBC).

2 – Intellectual Property

This includes all the details of your trademark type, trademark name, registering trademark office, and the registration number of your brand.

3 – Identification

This one includes your product images, brand logo/s, packaging images, and website/social media pages.

4 – Characteristics

This one includes your seller account information, vendor account details, barcodes, and manufacturing details like where it is made & distributed.

You have to complete all of these details for you to get approval.

Step 4 – Verification

Wait for 1-2 weeks in which Amazon will forward your brand's details to the registered trademark office. This office will then forward a code to you which you will have to send back to Amazon for verification.

You can do this step by going to:

Amazon Seller Central - > Enter the Respective **Case ID - > Go Button**

Select the **Respond or View Button** - > **Choose Reply** - > Paste the Code and click **Send.**

If you need more help on getting approved, I highly recommend that you contact Amazon's support as I found them to be really helpful for this process.

Sales Boost Idea #11 - Win Amazon's Buy Box

Around 83% of all Amazon sales comes through the Buy Box. That means, if you're not winning the Buy Box, then you're not really making a killing with your product. Which also means winning the buy box is equal to getting 5x more sales than what you usually make.

If you're not familiar with the buy box, it's basically the Add to Cart and the Buy Button on the right side of an Amazon listing. If you look further down on that part, you will most likely see other vendors selling the same product you are selling.

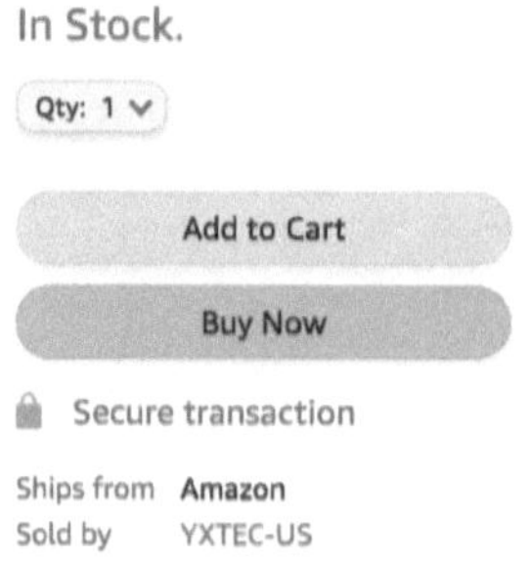

[Image 1.14]

(This particular buy box was won by YXTEC-US)

[Image 1.15]

(The other 6 sellers are available but only 17% of people on average look at them)

83% of the people who will buy the product won't even consider looking at the other vendors available. They will most likely purchase from the one who already has the buy box.

So how do you win the buy box? What are the things that you can do so Amazon will favor you as the winner?

A – Inventory

You should always replenish your inventory on time. The less problems you have with inventory availability, the better your chances of getting the buy box.

B - Fast Shipping

Fast shipping is a necessity these days. People are not willing to wait for more than 5 days anymore. Make sure that your items always arrive on time.

C - Customer-Service

You must also have an impeccable & prompt customer service. Answer any questions that they may have and always be polite when talking to customers.

D - Use of FBA/Professional Seller Account

You must have a professional seller's account or you'll have almost no chance of getting the buy box. Also, using FBA helps you with the last 2 metrics (fast shipping and customer service) since Amazon will do those 2 for you.

E - Competitive Pricing

Remember Amazon's mission: **To provide the widest selection at the lowest price.** That means Amazon wants you to provide cheaper prices compared to the competition.

F – Brand Registry/Enhance Brand Content

Registering for Brand Registry also helps in letting Amazon know that your brand and the products you sell are of the highest quality in the market.

G – Seller Rating

Amazon has 0 to 11 seller rating system and the higher your rating is, the more likely you are to get the buy box.

You cannot really control this one, so all you can do is try to provide the best product and respond to customers' inquiries as fast as possible.

Also, make sure that you have less than 1% product defect rate so you won't get penalized by Amazon.

***

There are obviously no guarantees when it comes to Amazon's decisions, but the more you follow these 7 key aspects, the better your chances of winning the buy box.

Sales Boost Idea #12 - Classify Your Products in the Right Category

Did you know that customers are 8.9% more likely to buy a product if they're in the right category? True story. I mean, Amazon said so.

Here's a shortcut in making sure that your product is in its right classification/category.

Look at your competitors' category and copy them.

If you're selling some kinesiology tape, then find your closest competitors and just look at what category they are using.

Product details

Color: Black - Precut

Date First Available : October 18, 2013

Manufacturer : KT Tape

ASIN : B08C5C57JD

Best Sellers Rank: #1,020 in Health & Household (See Top
#1 in Athletic Tapes & Wraps
#1 in Kinesiology Recovery Tapes

Customer Reviews:
★★★★☆ ˅   13,582 ratings

[Image 1.16]

Just copy the categories that they are using and classify your products on the same category inside your Seller Central Account.

Amazon will also automatically recommend other categories that you might want to use.

You can use Amazon's product classifier here:

<u>https://sellercentral.amazon.com/hz/inventory/classify</u>

Here are the instructions directly from Amazon (I'm putting it here for your convenience):

Step 1: Select your products' classifications

Go to the Product Classifier tool and use either the Browse or Search method to identify the appropriate classifications for your products.

Browse

1. Select the store in which your product belongs.
2. Continue to narrow the classification options until the Select button appears.
3. Click Select to add the classification to your list.
4. Repeat the process to classify all of your products.
5. Click Download List, and save the file.

Search

1. Type a keyword into the Search box.
2. Click the "+" (plus) sign to the left of the category name to select classifications for your products.
3. Repeat the process to classify all of your products.
4. Click Download List, and save the file.

[Image 1.17]

Step 2: Download the inventory file template

To identify the correct Inventory File Template:

1. Open the Product Classifier file and identify the inventory file template for your products by reviewing the suggestions in the Inventory Template Name column.
2. Go to Inventory File Templates, and download and save the inventory file or files. You can use more than one inventory file.

Note: For sellers using XML feeds, you can use an XML upload.

Step 3: Populate the classification and refinement fields

To add your selected classifications and refinements to your inventory file template files:

Classification

1. Open the Product Classifier file, and scroll to the Fields Required for Classification columns: Classification Field and Valid Values columns.
2. Identify the Classification Field for one of the products you are listing.
3. Identify these same fields in your inventory file template.

Note: item_type_keyword in the Product Classifier file corresponds to item_type in the Inventory File Template and the ItemType attribute in XML files

4. Copy the Valid Values from the Product Classifier file into the corresponding cell in the inventory file template for the product

[Image 1.18]

4. Copy the Valid Values from the Product Classifier file into the corresponding cell in the inventory file template for the product you are listing.

5. Repeat this process for all of the products you are listing.

Refinement:

1. Open the Product Classifier file, and scroll to the Refinements columns: Refinement Name, Refinement Field, Valid Values, and Modifier.

2. Identify the Refinement Field for one of the products you are listing.

3. Identify these same fields in your inventory file template.

4. Copy the Valid Values from the Product Classifier file into the corresponding cell in the inventory file template for the product you are listing.

5. Repeat this process for all of the products you are listing.

[Image 1.19]

You can also find it here:

https://sellercentral.amazon.com/gp/help/external/20157 6420

Sales Boost Idea #13 - Use Fulfillment by Amazon

I know, this may have been the most obvious sales boost idea in this book. But if you're still not using FBA by now, then the first thing that you have to do is to put down this book, go to your Seller Central account and sign-up for the FBA program.

The FBA program is probably the most genius thing ever when it comes to e-commerce. With FBA, I don't have to worry about shipping the product to the individual and I also don't have to worry about customer service since Amazon will take care of this for me. This saves me so much time that I can spend with my family and other parts of my business as well.

Sure, you have to pay some fees but it's well worth the investment because Amazon can ship so much faster than what I can do as an individual. When it comes to e-commerce, FAST SHIPPING is one of the keys to success and Amazon has the capability to do it the fastest.

If you want to know the nitty gritty on how you can find suppliers and ship your product to Amazon's warehouse, then I highly recommend that you check out my book FBA Product Sourcing Blueprint.

https://www.amazon.com/gp/product/B08NNTXHM9

Part 2

Product Based Ideas

Sales Boost Idea #14 - Sell Other Products and Establish a Brand

If you want to make as much money as possible, then you have to sell other products as well. Think of your product line up as an army of brand evangelists. A few months ago, I bought a body wash from a semi-unknown brand and mygod, I freaking love it. Can you guess what I did next? I checked out all their other lineups from shampoo, shaving cream, facewash, etc. I was so happy with one of their products that I decided to use that brand exclusively.

Imagine if I searched for their brand and the only product they are selling is that one body wash? I would've been disappointed because I really love the first product that I bought from them.

Obviously, in the beginning, you cannot have a product line up – but once you started growing, the next step is to expand and create and sell other products related to your first one.

This is how you build a successful e-commerce brand. You create one great product after another and then you dominate your market one new loyal customer at a time.

KEYS TO REMEMBER:

#1 – Sell Other Related/Complementary Products

Your next products should be complementary products that your original customers can buy. If you're selling a bamboo toothbrush, then sell a bamboo toothbrush case. If you're selling shampoo for men, then sell body wash for men for your next one.

#2 – Bundle Your Products

Another thing that you can do is to create a bundle and sell your products as a set. This will increase your average order and profit at the same time.

#3 – Great/Differentiated Product is Key

At the end of the day, your product must do what it promises to do. The only reason I got converted as a customer is because I love the first product that I bought. This is the key to your success with e-commerce, you must have a product with added value. If not, then you're just going to be a copycat and you will be out of business by this time next year.

Sales Boost Idea #15 - Drive Reviews and Customer Loyalty with Product Inserts

Getting more reviews is one of the most important type of marketing that you could ever do. More reviews mean more social proof that you have a great product. This is where product inserts come in. Aside from reviews, there's also a ton more other benefits that you could get from using them as well.

A product insert is basically a card (or a piece of paper) that you put inside the package that acts as an additional marketing material.

The intention is to communicate something with your customers. And that something could be the following:

1 – Get Feedback/Reviews. Customer reviews will always be the lifeblood of our products. Without them, we won't have any social proof that shows that our product is the best in the market.

2 – Customer Appreciation. You can also show appreciation for purchasing your product by simply saying "Thank You" or putting some kind of heartfelt message to your customers.

3 – Discount Codes. Offering discount codes via insert cards is a surefire way to get additional sales.

4 – Additional Instructions. If you're product is a little complicated or it require some additional instructions, an

insert is where you could put that additional text so they can maximize the use of the product.

5 – Promote Other Products. You can also mention other products that you have via an insert card, although in this case, you might want to put a bigger one instead of your classic 3 x 5 or 4 x 6 ones.
Note - Remember that you cannot do the following when it comes to product inserts:

1 – You cannot promote websites. NEVER re-direct your customers to your website. If you're going to promote a product, make sure that you mention that they should go to your Amazon store.

2 – Do not offer discounts and ask for reviews at the same time. NEVER offer discount codes and ask for a review at the same time. For your insert card, you can either ask for a sale via a discount code or you can ask for a review instead. You cannot combine them together in just one card.

3 – Do not use low quality papers. Your customers care about what you put in the package. Low quality papers easily get crumpled which makes the card looks less appealing.

4 – Do not divert the customers outside Amazon except if it's your social media properties like Facebook page or Instagram account.

5 – Do not specifically ask for a "positive/5-star review." This is against Amazon's TOS as well.

Here are some examples of awesome product inserts:

[Image 1.17]

[Image 1.18]

[Image 1.19]

Always err on the safe side. Yes, you can probably get away from incentivizing reviews, offering discounts for reviews, and re-directing customers to your website but I personally wouldn't risk it.

Whenever you're in doubt, always read Amazon's updated Terms of Service.

https://sellercentral.amazon.com/gp/help/G200386250

Sales Boost Idea #16 - Drive Sales with Product Inserts

Another awesome benefit of a product insert is you can drive additional sales from customers who already love you (assuming of course that you have a good product).

Here's how you can drive more sales through product inserts.

Step 1 – Thank You Message. Most seller just put a simple "Thank You" message and in most cases, that's actually pretty fine already. However, if you want to take it to the next level – adding a 2-3 sentence message saying how much you appreciate their support and how their patronage means a lot to your family owned business.

Step 2 – Mention Other Related Products. After saying thank you, you can then mention other related products that your store has.

Step 3 – Ask Them to Go to Your Amazon Store and Mention Your Brand.

Step 4 – Offer a Discount Code. Make sure that this code is only limited to 1 per customer.

In most cases, combining Step 1 and Step 4 is enough to get an increase of 20% in your sales every month.

Example of a good product insert that drive sales:

[Image 1.20]

As you can see on image 1.20, you can use the left one to drive sales, and then the right one to drive reviews. I wouldn't put them on one package as that may be in the gray area of Amazon's term of service.

The example on the left is probably the best example I can give when It comes to driving additional sales. It's simple, it's clean and it's direct to the point.

Here are more awesome ones to copy:

[Image 1.21]

[Image 1.22]

[Image 1.23]

Key things to remember:

1 – Do not direct your customers to your email, funnel, website or any web properties outside Amazon.com. Your social media pages are perfectly fine.

2 – You can offer a discount code but remember not to ask for a review at the same time. This is against Amazon's TOS.

Sales Boost Idea #17 - Offer Product Differentiation (Value Skewing)

I want to introduce you to the concept of value-skewing. It's basically about adding value to a product by being different and by giving what the customers are asking for. By adding value to the product, you'll be able to increase your sales and make your customers happy at the same time. It's a win-win situation for you and your customers.

Here's How to Differentiate via Value-Skewing:

1 – Materials and/or Ingredients.

You can use, not only better and higher quality ingredients but also materials and ingredients that your customers value. For example, if your customers are "ingredients sensitive" – they might prefer stevia over sugar. Stevia is healthier and it's a great substitute for sugar. In this case, changing an ingredient increases the value of your product in your customers eyes.

2 – Colors.

Adding different colors increases their options. There's a reason why the iPhone has different hues and colors for their devices. It's good for business and the customers want variety of options.

3 – Sizes.

Another way to add value is by adding sizes. There's no such thing as one size fits all. One t-shirt size cannot fit us all. One shoe size isn't enough. Offer different sizes and you'll be able to cater to a wider audience.

4 - Additional Features (via Research).

This will depend on the type of product you are selling. But there's always that one or two feature that customers are always looking for on a specific product. The best way to find these features is to read Amazon reviews and discover what customers are actually asking for.

5 – Origin.

Most of the time, the origin/manufacturing country of the product is a value-add in itself. There's a reason why Made in America or Made in Italy or Made in "Insert Country Here" matters in customers' buying decision.

But this still depends on the type of product you are selling. The general rule here is "the more expensive the product is, the better it is if it's *made in U.S.A., other Western Countries + Highly Reputable Manufacturing countries like Japan*" – and I'm not saying this because it's 100% true all of the time. I'm saying this because this is what the customers ASSUME (in general). The truth is, a product made from China can have higher quality than a product made in the U.S. However, this is not the current narrative that the market believes. Until this change, the origin of a product will continue to have an impact on customers' product preferences.

6 – Branding.

Another way to differentiate is through branding. By having a compelling story for your brand, you'll be able to change your customer's perception of your product. Branding is a complicated topic and I can write a whole book about it. But when it comes to e-commerce branding, the most important stuff are the following:

A – Always use social proof. This could be in the form of product reviews and/or endorsement from reputable users.
B – Start using video in your marketing.
C – Having the highest quality product is *branding done right* in itself.

7 – Packaging.

Your product's packaging affects how your product is seen in the market. Always use high quality materials in your packaging and try to give them an unboxing experience if possible. Look at what Apple is doing in their products, there's a reason why unboxing videos are getting millions of views online – customers love a good unboxing experience!

8 – Bonuses/Add-ons/Bundle.

Customers want more options so adding some kind of bonus/add-ons or even bundling a product can add profit to your bottom-line. Add-ons are always a good idea as long as it is actually adding value to what the customers are purchasing.

We will discuss some of these in detail on the next few chapters... Keep reading!

Sales Boost Idea #18 - Offer Purchase Add-ons + Multi-Packs

Remember that the best add-ons are complementary products.

For example, if you're selling a shaving razor then you might want to sell other products related to the razor.

As an example, let's look at what SHAVING REVOLUTION offers…

https://www.amazon.com/s?k=SHAVING+REVOLUTION

This company also offers: Double Edge Safety Razor, Stand, Bowl, After-Shave Balm, Pre-Shave Oil, and Badger Brush.

By having an add-on of other products that complements the original purchase, they can easily increase their sales and profit margin.

Remember that it's easier to sell to a customer that is already sold in the idea of buying one of your products. In this case, offering other stuff that may enhance their experience is in fact, not only more profitable but is also the right thing to do.

MULTI-PACKS

You can also offer what we call "multi-packs" and sell them by the number. 1 Pack, 2 Packs, 3 Packs, and so on are the usual. For example, instead of selling 1-piece of shaving soap, you can offer 5 pieces in 1-pack. And then you can do 2-packs, 3-packs and so on. The appeal of a pack is they can save money by buying bulk plus they don't have to worry about shipping fees over and over again. Try this simple strategy and see the results for yourself!

Sales Boost Idea #19 - Offer Gift Wrapping Options

Okay, technically – you're not really going to get a share of the profit for gift wrapping – but you should still offer it and enable it on Amazon.

Why? Because it offers a better customer buying experience. A lot of people buy products because they want to give it as a gift to someone they care about, and a lot of them also want the option to have it gift wrap. Remember, happy wife, happy life – oh wait – that's a different book – just change "wife" to "customers" and it's still true!

The actual price of the gift wrap will depend on how big the item is but you don't really have to worry about this since the customers will shoulder the cost for it.

If you're in FBA, then Amazon will automatically offer this service for your product. If it isn't, then you can go to your Seller Central account and go to **Settings**, then click **Gift Options**.

Click Edit next to **Gift** Messaging or **Gift-Wrap**, then enable the service for individual order items. Click Continue to save the setting.

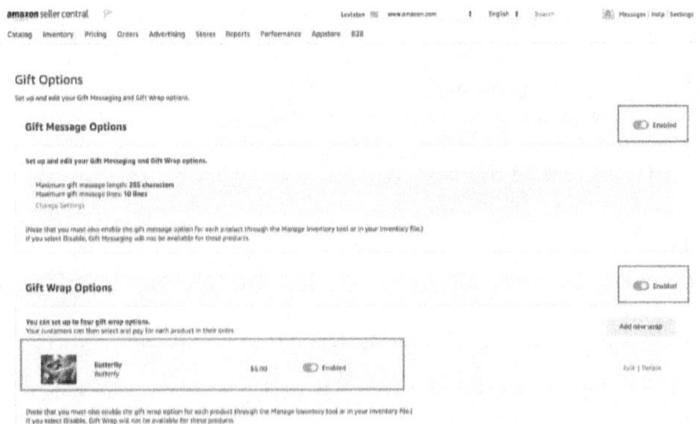

[Image 1.24]
[Image from Gorillaroi]*

Sales Boost Idea #20 - Read Competitors' Product Reviews and Improve Based on Customer Feedback

If you want to maximize the effect of value-skewing, then you have to know what your customers' most valued features [want and need] on a specific product. The best way to do this is to read your competitors' product reviews on Amazon and take note of what the customers are saying – both the positive and the negative stuff.

Let's say that you want to sell your own brand of Single-Blade Razor.

Here are the steps that I would take to research this product.

Step 1 – Search on Amazon.

I'll search for my closest competitors by searching for keywords like:

Single edge razor

Single blade razor

Step 2 – Read the Q & A section to find out customers' concerns.

When you read the Q & A section, try to find questions that appears over and over again on different products. By doing this, you'll know exactly what the common concerns are when it comes to this type of product.

In this case, I found the following concerns to be important for this market:

A – Where is the razor made? (major concern for this market*)

B – How many shaves can you get from one blade? (the more the better)

C – Does it come with blades? (they don't want to spend money on a razor that doesn't come with free blades)

By reading the Q & A section of different listings, I'd get to have an idea of their major concerns when buying a single edge razor.

Step 3 – Read the 1-star to 2-star reviews and find out about their concerns and what they didn't like about the product.

Step 4 – Read the 4 to 5-star reviews and find out what they like about the product.

Step 5 – Create a list and collect these concerns/comments.

Make sure that you put all your research into one document so you can refer to it as you source your product.

Step 6 – Create a better product that solves their concerns.

This is where all the research comes into fruition.

In order to create a product that gives you the best chance of winning the market, you have to solve the problems that you found on your research.

If your potential customers hate "China made razor", can you offer on that is locally made? Would it still make sense financially speaking? If yes, then this is a value-skew that you can turn in your favor.

If your customers prefer a single edge razor with matte grippable razor, can you offer this to them as an added value for your product?

This is not just about one feature, it's about adding value stack after another so you can become the preferred solution for your market's problems.

All of these starts with a simple product research on Amazon.

Sales Boost Idea #21 - Offer Different Product Colors and/or Sizes

This is probably the easiest value-skew that you can do since it doesn't really take that much effort on your part.

Customers will always have different preferences and needs when it comes to colors and sizes. There's a reason why there's different sizes of shoes, t-shirts, mobile devices, etc.

We want and need variety because there's no one size fits all.

When it comes to colors and sizes, you can try to go against the grain or just go with the flow.

For example, if you're selling a t-shirt, then people would expect that you'll have the classic colors like white, back, and grey.

If you're selling an aluminum razor, then you should probably have the classic matte or the mirror polished one. Then you can also use different touches like rose gold, jet black, and matte black to add a little flair to your product.

When it comes to color, try to follow the current trend if possible. For example, "rose gold" and "matte black" has been a big hit for Apple in the past few years and these colors had been ingrained to us as cool and hip. If possible, try to incorporate these colors to your products so you can have something attractive to offer your customers.

Sales Boost Idea #22 - Offer Bundles

This is one of my top value-skew to offer. Why?

Because it's a value-skew that helps you make more profit and makes your customers' save money at the same time.

When it comes to bundles, always think about what the customers need aside from your main product. Think about products that will complement your main one.

If you're selling a premium razor, then you may want to sell shaving cream, post shave oil, a brush, moisturizer, face wash, etc.

[Image 1.25]

Another bundle idea I recommend is the "Bundle 1 2 3 Strategy"

Instead of putting all of your available products in just 1 big bundle, you can create different types of bundles that will give your customers more options.

For example, Supplyco offers a "Starter Kit" with the razor, shaving cream, post shave healing, and shaving brush. That is bundle #1.

[Image 1.26]

But they also offer other smaller bundles that includes some of the same products, which we can call bundle #2 and bundle #3.

Obviously, you can change the name with something cooler but you get the point. ☺

See the image below for an example.

[Image 1.27]

Note: When it comes to the number of unique items inside your biggest bundle, I recommend that you put no more than 6 items inside. For your smaller bundles, 2-3 items per bundle is the usual practice.

Sales Boost Idea #23 - Offer Premium Product Options

There is a market for cheap and affordable items, just like there will always be a market for premium products.

So how would I approach this?

I would personally create a different brand if I offer a lot of other premium products. However, if it's only 1 or 2 items, I would just put it under the same brand. This will automatically increase the value of my other "cheaper" products.

Let's say that you are selling a mid-priced $50 razor. You can come up with a more expensive razor at the price range of $150-$200. Now, you shouldn't expect to make a lot of sales for this one but you can still make a decent profit from it. At the same time, this also increases the value of your cheaper products. Most people can't afford a $200 razor, so they would go for the next best thing which is your cheaper, but still perfectly awesome $50 alternative.

This is what Zafirro did with their razors (although this one is to the total extreme).

They offered a razor made of gold for $18,000 and one made of iridium for $100,000.

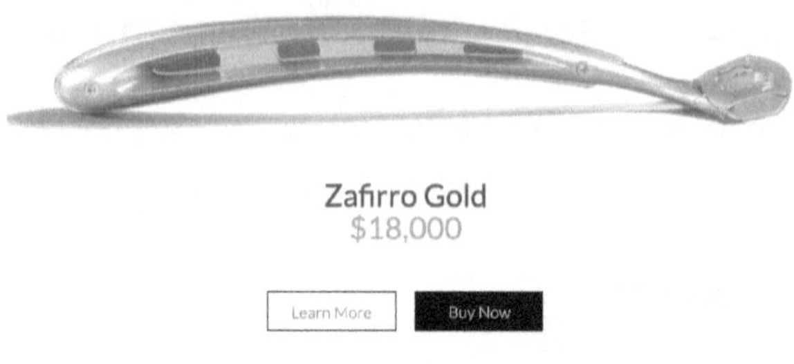

[Image 1.28]

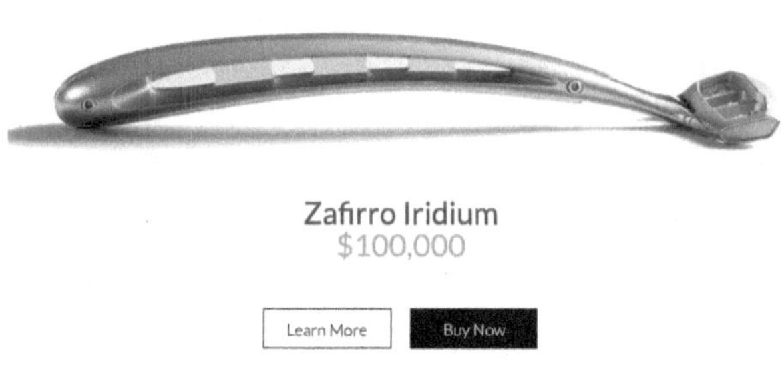

[Image 1.29]

Then they offer the "Zafirro Z2" at $199 which is still quite expensive for a razor. But because of their 2 other products, $199 seems like a bargain now in comparison to their original offerings.

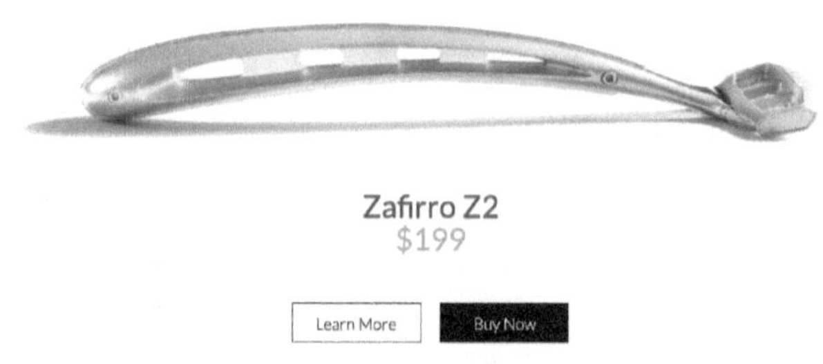

[Image 1.30]

You don't have to source thousands of your premium product, a few hundred (especially in the beginning) will do.

Honestly, it doesn't really take more effort to sell a more expensive product. You can pretty much use the same tactics that you learned from this book so far. The only major difference is you'll probably have to advertise and promote a little bit more than usual.

That's where the next part comes in. Marketing and Promotion are key aspects of every business, especially the ones that are still trying to make a name for their brands.

Now, remember that these advertising and promotion techniques are all useless if you don't have a good product and if you didn't optimize your Amazon listing for maximum sales. Focus on those 2 aspects first before you dive right into ads and promotions.

Part 3

Marketing & Promotion

Sales Boost Idea #24 - Advertise on Amazon

Okay, first of all I'm not going to teach you the technical aspect of advertising on Amazon here. You can learn that easy peasy stuff through Amazon's blog: https://advertising.amazon.com/en-us/blog.

What I want to teach you are the most important stuff that you have to remember when you're advertising on Amazon. Think of these as the best practices to follow when you start advertising your products. The more of these you follow, the more likely you are to gain higher profits.

MY TOP 7 AMAZON ADS BEST PRACTICES:

#1 - Start with $3-$5 Budget Per Day

You don't have to start with $20 or even $50 per day budget. The first 3-4 weeks of your ads should be spent testing campaigns and finding out what works. Not all of us have thousands of dollars for an ad campaign, but we can all run 3-4 campaigns at $3 per day per campaign.

#2 – Start with 3 Ads (Manual and Automatic)

When you start running ads, DO NOT try to run different ad creatives or copy. Just create one ad copy and make the AUDIENCE your key variable.

That means running 1 automatic campaign, 1 manual with all your main keywords, and another one with all your broad keywords. You should run these campaigns for 2-3 weeks without changing anything.

#3 – Use Your Keyword List

A keyword list is basically a master file that consists of all the keywords that you can use for your listing so you can rank higher on Amazon's search engine. You can also use these keywords for Amazon ads and Google ads. If you don't have this master keyword list yet, I recommend that you check out the 3rd part of this series called Amazon Keyword Research.

As a starter, I recommend that you gather your main keywords by searching for products related to yours on Amazon and then grab the keywords that are most related to what you're selling.

#4 – Use Amazon Dynamic Bids – Down Only

Always start with this bidding option so you don't overpay for ads.

#5 – Start with Amazon's Bid Recommendation and Don't Change Anything for 2 Weeks

For the amount of bid, start with what Amazon recommends and then don't change anything for two weeks. Amazon's algorithm takes time and changing things brings confusion to the system. Just stick with what you already have and **let the machines do the work**. Out of the 3 campaigns that you got, one will likely be a clear winner after 2-3 weeks and you'll know which ad audience works best for you.

#6 – Don't Stop the Campaign if 1-2 Sales Can Put You in the Green

If 1 or 2 sales will put you to positive ROI, then don't stop the campaign just yet. Keep running it for another week or two and see if it will turn itself around. Most of my successful campaigns didn't start profitable. They all need that time so Amazon can find the best audience for my product.

#7 – Scale by Duplicating Profitable Campaigns

Once you found that winning/profitable campaign, do not scale the ad by 5x'ing your budget. If you're running a $5 per day ad, then you should only max out the per day budget up to $20. You should scale instead by creating a similar campaign with only 1 tiny difference. I recommend that you change just one thing and then start running that ad as well. Most of the time, I'll just remove 1 or 2 keywords that are spending but not really making any profit.

Sales Boost Idea #25 - Use Facebook Ads

The great thing about Facebook Ads is you can target via a specific demographic or interests. In addition, you can collect email address that you can use for your long-term ecommerce success. And even more awesome is you can test different ad creatives like images and videos. In short, you're not limited unlike on Amazon.

So, should you directly send customers to your Amazon Listing?

Frankly, I do not recommend it. Amazon ads can get expensive if your product doesn't have the best profit margin. In this case, you have to play the long game and get as many emails as you can while also selling the product at the same time.

Here's the strategy I recommend:

Ad - > Landing Page - > Listing

Start with a Facebook Ad, send them to a landing page with a discount coupon, and then send them to your Amazon listing after they signed up for the discount code. With this strategy, you'll be able to collect their email and send them to your listing at the same time.

My Ad Recommendation:

VIDEO WORKS BEST. A simple 1-minute video showcasing your product's features and benefits is the best type of ad you can do right now.

Check out these links for an example:

DishFish:
https://www.youtube.com/watch?v=umnz-4ZlrEc&ab_channel=DishFish%E2%84%A2

Recurve Bows:
https://www.youtube.com/watch?v=4B12pqCX7LY&ab_channel=Camping%26Hiking

Roof Cleaner:
https://www.youtube.com/watch?v=OAxlRWHL-Vo&ab_channel=30SecondsLtd

MY TARGETING RECOMMENDATION:

Start with your main market. Use your common sense and market knowledge here. Who are your main customers? Are they men or women? Where do they live? What type of fan pages are they following on Facebook? You have to know these things and I would assume that you already did your research because you are already selling something in your chosen market.

My Landing Page Recommendation:

[Image 1.31]

For your landing page, I recommend a simple one that clearly mention what they are getting.

Start with the headline that says "Save Big on X [your product]"

Add a picture on the left side. Then on the right side, tell them exactly how much they are saving, plus add the button that lets them sign up for the coupon code.

You can use any of these landing page creators: WordPress (free), Leadpages, Clickfunnels, or Unbounce.

Once they signed up, send them the coupon code via email and then direct them to your Amazon listing so they could buy the product.

Sales Boost Idea #26 - Use Instagram to Increase Market Share

Instagram is still one of the most underutilized platform when it comes to e-commerce. The goal for Instagram marketing isn't really to make quick-sales, the goal should be about building a brand people love and trust.

So, this isn't exactly a "quick sales boost idea."

Nonetheless, I still recommend that you create a brand that is active on Instagram because it will separate your products from the thousands of competitors that you have.

You already know that when it comes to Instagram, high-quality images are the key. That's pretty obvious. But what are you supposed to have other than that?

#1 – Use Variety of Content

Always go for variety of content. You can post about your products directly promoting them, you can post a quote related to your product, a customer testimonial, fun facts, behind the scenes, and other video content. The key here is to post as much variety as you can.

#2 – Encourage User-Generated Content

This one is going to play a major role in your brand's ability to dominate a market. Just about every brand that is killing it on Instagram right now are using user-generated content. Always encourage your customers to post your product on Instagram, and then re-post them so you can use it as content. Being featured makes your customers appreciate your brand more thus making them an evangelist for your products.

#3 – Use the Right Hashtags

Don't just use random hashtags that has nothing to do with your post. Always research the most important ones that are related to what you're sharing. There's nothing more annoying to an IG user than finding images of non-related pictures when they're searching for a hashtag they like to explore.

#4 – Interact with Your Followers

Lastly, you want to interact with your followers as much as possible. In the beginning, I recommend that you like and reply every single comment that you will get on your page. This is going to be harder once you already have thousands of followers but you should still do it as much as possible. Replying on comments differentiates you from the corporate pirates who only cares about their profits. Be different and actually take the time to create even a small connection with your customers.

Sales Boost Idea #27 - Find & Work with Influencers

I know, I know... everyone seems like an influencer nowadays and it is hard to find someone who can truly be a good influencer for your brand.

Here's what I recommend that you do:

Step 1 – Know Who Your Audience Is

You have to know who your audience is. What hashtags are they following? What type of videos are they watching? What type of content are they into? Knowing exactly what type of stuff your audience is into will maximize the effect of an influencer (even the ones with only 5,000 to 30,000 followers).

Step 2 – Find the Right Medium

The next step is to choose the right medium. What's the best platform that you can use in order to achieve your goals? This will depend on what you want. Do you want to increase brand awareness? Do you want to get as much sales as possible? Create the right expectation so you can achieve the most desirable results. Then choose a platform that would best serve your intentions. You can choose between Instagram, TikTok, YouTube, Twitter, or Facebook.

Step 3 – Find and Work with the Right Influencer

To find influencers to work with, I recommend that you use BuzzSumo's influencer search tool.

https://buzzsumo.com/find-influencers/

There's a 30-day free trial and that should be enough time for you to find awesome influencers you can work with.
If you have a relatively new brand and you don't have a big budget yet, I recommend that you focus on working with micro-influencers. These are influencers with 10k to 50k followers. They're cheaper and they will have higher conversions than those who already have hundreds of thousands of followers. Most micro-influencers will charge between $50 to $500 per post. So, before you choose the ones you want to work with, make sure that you check the following first:

A – Engagement. They should be active in interacting with their followers.
B – Specialization. You should choose someone who clearly specialize on the type of product you want to promote.
C – Reach. Go for the ones with less than 50,000 followers if you're just getting started with Influencer marketing.

I highly recommend that you check-out this informative article about the ins and outs of Influencer marketing:

https://influencermarketinghub.com/influencer-rates/

Step 4 – Track Your Campaigns

Always use some kind of unique coupon or trackable unique link so you know exactly how many people are buying your product through the Influencer's recommendation. A discount code is my go-to option since they're much easier to track.

Sales Boost Idea #28 - Use Amazon's Early Reviewer Program

We all know the importance of Amazon product reviews by now.

More reviews, means more social proof, which typically leads to more sales. And no product reviews, means no sales, and no sales means you don't get any reviews – it's the classic what comes first? Egg or chicken.

So how in the world can you get reviews?

Remember, you cannot purchase or exchange reviews – that would be against Amazon's Terms of Service.

This is where **Amazon Early Reviewer Program** comes in.

What it does is it allows you to get at least 5 initial reviews for your brand-new product.

But first, you have to find out if you are eligible for the program.

Here are some of the requirements according to Amazon:

- The product must be for sale on Amazon.com or Amazon.co.uk
- You have to have a brand registry
- The product must have less than 5 reviews when you apply for the program
- The product cost must be at least $15
- It must have its own SKU barcode

The Price

Is it worth the $60 that you have to pay for? I believe so. A product that has at least 5 reviews is 2.5x more likely to get sales than the one without any.

Go on and apply your product to the Early Reviewer Program because it's the best $60 you'll ever spend this week.

*To **participate**, submit your product via 'Seller Central > Advertising > **Early Reviewer Program**'. You can submit single SKUs directly via the **Amazon Early Reviewer Program** dashboard.*

Sales Boost Idea #29 - Apply for Lightning Deals

Doing an Amazon Lightning Deal is one of the best ways to gain market visibility and increase your product sales on Amazon. It also allows you to get a leap against the competition and it gives you the chance to sustain it by increasing your best-seller rankings.

Amazon Lightning Deals are pretty straightforward. You apply to be included in a lightning deal, Amazon promotes the deal, and your product gets discounted for no more than 6 hours.

Eligibility

Here are the requirements for approval:

- You must be a "professional" seller
- Your product must be receiving at least 5 reviews per month
- You must have a seller rating of at least 3.5 stars
- The product must have an average rating of at least 3 stars
- A product with variations is a plus
- Your product shouldn't be in the non-eligible categories like e-cigarettes, medical devices, alcohol, and adult products

How to Apply for a Lightning Deal

Log-in to your Seller Central panel - > Select the Create tab - > Pick the One You Want a Deal for - > click Edit - >

fill the needed information like schedule, minimum price, and minimum deal quantity.

You can monitor the status of your application through the Lightning Deal Dashboard.

The fee to join varies, but the average would be around $150. It's definitely worth the price since you'll be getting an avalanche of sales plus this would be great for your product in the long-term.

Think of the sales for the deal as a bonus.

The real benefit of lightning deals is you'll get the chance to get more sales after the deal since your product will have a much higher best-seller ranking and more people will see and buy from your listing.

Sales Boost Idea #30 - Make Your Products Amazon Prime Eligible

Consider prime as a gift from the e-commerce gods, or maybe Jeff Bezos – who knows. All I know is that being an Amazon Prime eligible seller is awesome!

For the buyer, they get free shipping, discounts and other promos.

For the sellers, you will get a prime badge which is crucial nowadays on Amazon. It means you're in the cool club with the cool kids – and in this case, the cool kids are buying a lot of stuff on Amazon.

How to Join Amazon Prime:

Option #1 - Self-Fulfilled Prime. If you store and ship your own products, you can still join prime via SFP. You need to join the waitlist at the moment since they're not openly accepting members.

You'll be put into a trial mode and you're going to have to perform tasks that is up to par to their standards.

You can join the waitlist here:

https://sell.amazon.com/programs/seller-fulfilled-prime.html

Option #2 - Join Amazon FBA. If you're already an FBA seller, then you don't have to worry anymore. All you have to do is maintain a good seller performance rating and you're in! (https://sellercentral.amazon.com/gp/help/external/G200 205250?language=en_US)

This is still the easiest way to be prime eligible, plus the fees are basically baked into your Amazon selling fees so you don't need to worry about that as well.

Joining Amazon Prime is probably the least effort activity you can do to increase your sales. This should be priority #1 as soon as you start selling your products on Amazon.

Sales Boost Idea #31 - Join Amazon's Subscribe & Save Program

Think of the Subscribe and Save program as Amazon's digital loyalty card. People get to save money by subscribing and you get to make consistent sales and profit by having subscriptions on the products you are selling.

This works best for products that are sold on a weekly/monthly basis. Products like food, toiletries, health products and most consumable stuff.

How to Join Subscribe and Save Program

Step 1 – Go to your FBA account's settings.

Step 2 – Locate **Subscription & Settings** and **Enable Subscribe and Save.**

Step 3 – Add the products that you want to include.

And voila! You're ready to sell your product subscription!

What I like about the S&S program is it runs forever. It's not liked a one-time lightning deal. With S&S, you get to do this thing once and you get to benefit from it forever.

In terms of long-term income, this is one of the best things you can do for your Amazon business.

Note: Check out this link below for some eligibility requirements

https://sellercentral.amazon.com/gp/help/external/G2016
20110?language=en_US

Sales Boost Idea #32 - Post Your Listing on Your Personal FB Profile

Okay, this may seem like a trivial thing to do but if you're just getting started – you must do everything in your power to promote your products. And that includes sharing them on your Facebook profile.

A simple post sharing the link of your product/s will do. Let your friends know that your company produces these products and ask them to check it out if it's something that they want or need.

That's it. Simple, but actually quite effective for getting a few sales every now and then.

Sales Boost Idea #33 - Expand to International Markets

Amazon Global Selling is definitely not for everyone. However, if you have a product that is selling quite well in the U.S., then there's a good chance that it could be a hit for other markets as well. Obviously, there are no guarantees since every market is different, but it wouldn't hurt to try and sell your best-selling product on international marketplaces.

I recommend that you start with Amazon.co.uk since Western culture will still be prevalent in this region and you'll still have almost the same demographic for your product.

The process is pretty much the same, except that you'll send your products on Amazon's international warehouse instead.

You can register for a UK seller central account here:

https://sellercentral.amazon.co.uk/

Some things to remember before you sell your products on Amazon UK:

1 – Check the legal implications and regulations of selling internationally.

2 – Check out your competition to know the average price of your product in the international scene.

3 – Always start small and test 20 to 100 pieces of your product first before you go all-in.

P.S. I will probably be writing a book about International markets like UK and Japan in the near future, so you may want to watch out for those books when they get released ☺

Conclusion

The rise of different work from home business ideas also gave rise to a lot of Amazon wannabe entrepreneurs. This means that the competition is now tougher than ever. A lot of new online entrepreneurs won't even be able to source a single product, but a part of those will be able to get their product to the Amazon marketplace. And that's where the battle begins. If you're in a place where you just launched your first product, then you must do everything in your power to become your own product evangelist. You must become your product's number one fan, at least in the beginning.

As you just discovered, there are 3 phases to increasing your Amazon sales. There's the optimization part where you deal with your listing – title, keywords, pricing, etc. Then there's the product part where you focus on improving your product as you gain more experience in your chosen market. Then the 3rd part, which is marketing your product for maximum sales. You don't necessarily have to treat it like steps 1 2 and 3. But I do recommend that you start with optimization and always be on the lookout for ways to improve your customer's buying experience.

Progress > Perfection

Before I let you go, I want to reiterate something that has been a huge part of my own Amazon mini-success story. And that is **progress is better than perfection.** Obviously, I'm not saying that you should just take random action and just keep breaking things. My point is that you should focus in applying the ideas inside this book as fast as possible while still doing them deliberately. 80% of the people who read this book will probably won't do anything with the information they gathered from it – the excuses will range from "it's too simple to work" or "it's too much work to bother," whatever your excuses are, I guarantee you that you won't make it in this business if all you do all day is complain about stuff that you have no control over. I'm sorry to be blunt and I'm sorry if I'm being mean to you right now, it's just that I've been writing these Amazon series for years now and I really hate seeing people fail when they could've easily done something about it.

My first book, "Amazon FBA for Beginners" is one of the most (if not the most) reviewed FBA book of all-time. I'm not saying that to brag. I'm saying that because I want you to know that because of the feedback I got from the reviewers, I am also heavily emotionally invested in the success of my readers. The reason why I keep writing these books is because I see how many lives can be changed if you just put your heart into something you think is important.

Go out there and produce quality products for your market, I guarantee you that that will be the best decision you'll ever make in your business.

Go prosper and see you on the other side,

Red

Review Request

If you like this book and it helped you in some way or another, I would like to request for you to kindly post a review on Amazon.com. Reviews are the lifeblood of every author out there and it helps in sharing the message.

I appreciate you and I look forward to hearing from you soon. Good luck on your business and I wish you all the success in the world.

Fulfillment by Amazon for Beginners

If you like to learn a simple and step by step way of getting started with Amazon FBA, I recommend that you check out my other books AMAZON FBA Step by Step (by Red Mikhail), FBA Product Research 101, Amazon Keyword Research 101, and FBA Product Sourcing Blueprint as well.

These are also available as audiobooks.

Just like this one, these 4 has a very simple language and conversational tone to it. If you found this book valuable, then you will like those 4 books as well.

OTHER BOOKS

I also have other books about making money online through different ways, check them out here:

Amazon's Associate Program

https://www.amazon.com/gp/product/B019EV4QA0/

One Hour Dropshipping System

https://www.amazon.com/gp/product/B014PU7S9Q

Amazon Product Listing Formula

https://www.amazon.com/gp/product/B0142ZWRC2

AMAZON FBA FUTURE UPDATES:

We're just scratching the surface. In the next few months (or years), I'm going to launch a series of books about:

FBA Advance Traffic & Marketing Strategies

Amazon Wholesaling

Amazon Retail Arbitrage

Amazon Dropshipping

And many more books related to starting and growing an Amazon ecommerce business.

If you want to make sure that you get a notification when these books go LIVE, just simply follow my Amazon author page here:

https://www.amazon.com/Red-Mikhail/e/B00X3KJ2TO/

(Click the follow button on that page to get instant updates from Amazon)

www.ingramcontent.com/pod-product-compliance
Lightning Source LLC
Chambersburg PA
CBHW021335060726
47591CB00006B/2027